muffins

and other morning bakes

muffins
and other morning bakes

Linda Collister

with photography by Philip Webb

RYLAND
PETERS
& SMALL

LONDON NEW YORK

To all the grandparents of my children.

Senior Designer	**Ashley Western**
Editor	**Maddalena Bastianelli**
Food Stylist	**Linda Collister**
Stylist	**Mary Norden**
Production	**Patricia Harrington**
Art Director	**Gabriella Le Grazie**
Publishing Director	**Alison Starling**

Notes: Before baking, always remember to weigh or measure all the necessary ingredients exactly and prepare baking tins or sheets. Ovens should be preheated to the specified temperature – if using a fan-assisted oven, cooking times should be reduced according to the manufacturer's instructions.

First published in Great Britain in 2000 as
Morning Bakes by Ryland Peters & Small
Kirkman House
12–14 Whitfield Street
London W1T 2RP
www.rylandpeters.com

This edition first published in 2003

10 9 8 7 6 5 4 3 2 1

ISBN 1 900518 99 6

A catalogue record for this book is available from the
British Library.

Printed and bound in China.

contents

introduction

In my ideal world, breakfast and morning treats would be made with love and care, so here are recipes for quick, nutritious weekday breakfasts as well as leisurely weekend brunches. These bakes use nuts and fresh or dried fruit for flavour and nutrition, and are lower in fat and sugar than many of their teatime cousins.

Baking depends on a few key ingredients and their quality determines the result. Luckily, even the best – and these are now usually organically grown – are relatively inexpensive: unsalted butter, free-range eggs, stoneground unbleached flour, untreated fruit, organic nuts, cocoa powder and chocolate. These days major supermarkets have an excellent range of organic foods.

Life can be simpler for the morning baker if you remember to take butter and eggs out of the fridge the night before so they are at room temperature when you

are ready to cook. Dry ingredients can be weighed and mixed in advance, bakeware prepared, even a special holiday breakfast table can be set ahead of time.

The quickest recipes are favourites with my small children – French toast and cinnamon toast have an enduring appeal and need no advance preparation. Pancakes and waffles are high on our list of instant treats – three generations of my husband's family have grown up on the gruesomely sticky combination of pancakes layered with peanut butter and maple syrup.

Muffins can also be easily assembled. They freeze well and can be reheated; add a fresh fruit compote and yoghurt for a really good combination. Muffins and quick breads go well with savouries like scrambled or poached eggs, omelettes, cold ham, crispy bacon or warm smoked haddock or – best of all – kippers.

Leftover quick breads are excellent toasted and buttered. Yeasted breads and loaf cakes take more time and planning, and baking ahead – this can work to your advantage. They also keep longer, and most freeze well.

cardamom, carrot and bran muffins

A healthy bran cereal breakfast – but in delicious muffin form, and just packed with spices and plump raisins.

Put the cereal in a large bowl, add the milk and let soak for 10 minutes. Lightly beat the eggs in another bowl and add to the soaked cereal mixture with the melted butter or oil. Stir well.

Add the dry ingredients, then stir quickly and briefly. Do not overmix; the mixture should be lumpy. Stir in the grated carrots and raisins, if using, then spoon into the prepared muffin tin, filling each hole about two-thirds full.

Bake in a preheated oven at 220°C (425°F) Gas 7 for about 20 minutes until lightly browned and firm to the touch. Let cool in the tin for 1 minute, then turn out onto a wire rack. Eat warm, immediately or within 24 hours. When thoroughly cooled, the muffins can be wrapped then frozen for up to 1 month.

80 g shredded bran cereal

230 ml milk

2 large eggs

4 tablespoons melted butter or vegetable oil

200 g plain flour, sifted

2½ teaspoons baking powder, sifted

⅛ teaspoon ground cardamom

75 g light muscovado sugar

150 g grated carrots

70 g raisins (optional)

a deep 12-hole muffin tin, well greased

Makes 12 muffins

muffins

Seville orange marmalade – everyone's favourite breakfast preserve – makes a gorgeous baking treat. Simple, easy-to-make muffins.

Sift the dry ingredients into a large bowl, mix thoroughly, then make a well in the centre. Add the egg, milk, orange juice and oil or melted butter. Stir the marmalade to break up any large clumps, then add to the bowl. Mix quickly to form a coarse, slightly streaky batter; do not overmix. Spoon the mixture into the prepared muffin tin, filling each hole about two-thirds full.

Bake in a preheated oven at 220°C (425°F) Gas 7 for 20 minutes until lightly browned and firm to the touch. Let cool in the tin for 1 minute, then turn out onto a wire rack. Eat warm, immediately or within 24 hours. When thoroughly cooled, the muffins can be wrapped then frozen for up to 1 month.

150 g plain flour

150 g wholemeal flour

1 tablespoon baking powder

a large pinch of sea salt

1 large egg, lightly beaten

280 ml milk

2 teaspoons freshly squeezed orange juice

4 tablespoons vegetable oil or melted butter

150 g thick-cut Seville orange marmalade

a deep 12-hole muffin tin, well greased

Makes 12 muffins

marmalade muffins

50 g whole blanched almonds

250 g plain flour, sifted

1 tablespoon baking powder, sifted

85 g golden caster sugar

grated rind of 1 unwaxed lemon

1 large egg

280 ml milk

2 teaspoons freshly squeezed lemon juice

4 tablespoons vegetable oil

150 g fresh blueberries, rinsed and
thoroughly drained, or frozen blueberries
(use straight from the freezer)

a deep 12-hole muffin tin, well greased

Makes 12 muffins

Put the almonds in a food processor or blender and grind to a coarse meal. They should have more texture than commercially ground almonds. Transfer to a large bowl and mix with the flour, baking powder, sugar and grated lemon rind.

Lightly beat the egg with the milk, lemon juice and vegetable oil. Add to the dry ingredients and stir just enough to make a coarse, lumpy mixture. Add the blueberries and mix quickly, using as few strokes as possible, leaving the mixture slightly streaky. Do not beat or overmix or the muffins will be tough and dry.

Spoon the mixture into the prepared muffin tin, filling each hole about two-thirds full. Bake in a preheated oven at 200°C (400°F) Gas 6 for about 20–25 minutes until golden and firm to the touch.

lemon, almond and blueberry muffins

Let cool in the tin for 1 minute, then turn out onto a wire rack. Eat warm, immediately or within 24 hours. When thoroughly cooled, the muffins can be wrapped then frozen for up to 1 month.

Everyone loves a blueberry muffin. These are extra special, packed with ground almonds. Use wild berries if you can find them.

pecan, orange and cranberry muffins

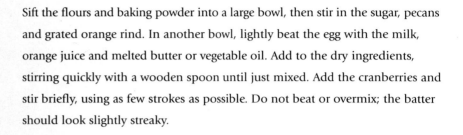

Sift the flours and baking powder into a large bowl, then stir in the sugar, pecans and grated orange rind. In another bowl, lightly beat the egg with the milk, orange juice and melted butter or vegetable oil. Add to the dry ingredients, stirring quickly with a wooden spoon until just mixed. Add the cranberries and stir briefly, using as few strokes as possible. Do not beat or overmix; the batter should look slightly streaky.

Spoon into the prepared muffin tin, filling each hole about two-thirds full. Bake in a preheated oven at 220°C (425°F) Gas 7 for about 20 minutes until golden brown and firm to the touch. Let cool in the tin for 1 minute, then turn out onto a wire rack. Eat warm, immediately or within 24 hours. When thoroughly cooled, the muffins can be wrapped then frozen for up to 1 month.

150 g plain flour
150 g wholemeal flour
1 tablespoon baking powder
85 g golden caster sugar
50 g pecans, coarsely chopped
grated rind of ½ unwaxed orange
1 large egg
280 ml milk
2 teaspoons freshly squeezed
    orange juice

4 tablespoons melted butter
    or vegetable oil
150 g fresh or frozen cranberries
    (use straight from the freezer)

a deep 12-hole muffin tin,
    well greased

Makes 12 muffins

fresh peach and oat muffins

115 g rolled oats

300 ml buttermilk

1 large egg, lightly beaten

6 tablespoons melted butter or
   vegetable oil

85 g light muscovado sugar

200 g plain flour

1 teaspoon baking powder

$\frac{1}{2}$ teaspoon bicarbonate of soda

$\frac{1}{2}$ teaspoon ground cinnamon

$\frac{1}{4}$ teaspoon grated nutmeg

2 almost ripe, medium peaches, rinsed,
   stoned and flesh cut into large chunks

a deep 12-hole muffin tin, well greased

Makes 12 muffins

Put the rolled oats and the buttermilk in a large bowl and let soak for 10 minutes. Add the lightly beaten egg, melted butter or vegetable oil and sugar and mix well.

Sift the flour, baking powder, bicarbonate of soda and spices onto the soaked oat mixture and stir briefly. Quickly fold in the chopped peaches. Do not beat or overmix; the batter should look slightly streaky. Spoon the mixture into the prepared muffin tin, filling each hole about two-thirds full.

Bake in a preheated oven at 220°C (425°F) Gas 7 for about 20–25 minutes until golden brown and firm to the touch. Let cool in the tin for 1 minute, then turn out onto a wire rack. Eat warm, immediately or within 24 hours. When thoroughly cooled, the muffins can be wrapped then frozen for up to 1 month.

Fresh peaches make these muffins special. Serve warm with fruit salad compote, plus Greek-style yoghurt or low-fat fromage frais.

125 g bacon, diced

150 g yellow cornmeal

150 g plain flour, sifted

¼ teaspoon coarsely ground black
pepper or crushed dried chillies

1 tablespoon baking powder, sifted

2 large eggs, lightly beaten

230 ml milk

1 tablespoon bacon fat (see recipe),
vegetable or sunflower oil

1 teaspoon maple syrup

1 tablespoon fresh herbs, such as snipped
chives or chopped parsley, or sliced spring
onions

a 12-hole deep muffin tin, well greased

Makes 12 muffins

Put the bacon into a cold frying pan, non-stick if possible, and fry until golden and crisp. Remove the bacon and transfer to a plate lined with crumpled kitchen paper. Drain off all but 1 tablespoon of the fat in the frying pan (if necessary, make up to this amount with vegetable or sunflower oil).

Put all the dry ingredients in a large bowl and mix. Add the crispy bacon, eggs, milk, bacon fat or oil, syrup and the herbs or spring onions. Mix quickly to make a coarse, slightly streaky batter. Do not beat or overmix. Spoon the mixture into the prepared muffin tin, filling each hole about two-thirds full. Bake in a preheated oven at 220°C (425°F) Gas 7 for about 15 minutes until lightly golden and just firm to the touch. Let cool in the tin for 1 minute, then turn out onto a wire rack. Eat warm, immediately or within 24 hours. When thoroughly cooled, the muffins can be wrapped then frozen for up to 1 month.

cornmeal and bacon muffins

Delicious with light, buttery scrambled eggs or omelettes, cold ham and tomatoes or a full English fried breakfast.

oat baps

The bap is one of the glories of British baking and in Scotland, the oat capital of the world, they are made with crunchy rolled oats.

Put the dry ingredients in a food processor and process to make a fairly coarse mixture. Mix the milk with the lemon juice, then with the machine running, slowly pour the liquid through the feed tube to make a soft but not sticky dough. Turn out onto a surface dusted with oats, then roll or pat into a round loaf about 23 cm in diameter and 5 cm thick.

Put the loaf on the prepared baking sheet and, using a sharp knife, score it into 8 wedges. Bake in a preheated oven at 190°C (375°F) Gas 5 for about 20 minutes until firm to the touch and lightly browned underneath. Cool on a wire rack. Eat warm, immediately, or split and toast. When thoroughly cooled, the baps can be wrapped then frozen for up to 1 month.

200 g rolled oats, plus extra for dusting

300 g plain flour

1 teaspoon sea salt

1 teaspoon bicarbonate of soda, sifted

400 ml full-fat milk

2 teaspoons freshly squeezed lemon juice

a large baking sheet, well greased

Makes 8 baps

quick breads

apple buttermilk scone round

Eat warm, spread with butter and lots of apricot preserve, pear and ginger jam or apple marmalade – a good start to the day.

Peel, core and coarsely chop the apple into 1-cm chunks. Mix the flours, bicarbonate of soda and sugar in a food processor. Add the chilled cubes of butter and process until the mixture looks like fine crumbs. With the machine running, add the buttermilk through the feed tube to make a soft but not sticky dough.

Turn out onto a floured surface and knead in the apple chunks to form a coarse and bumpy dough. Shape into a ball and put in the middle of the prepared baking sheet. With floured fingers, pat into a 22-cm round. Brush lightly with buttermilk or milk to glaze, then sprinkle with a little demerara sugar to give a crunchy surface. Using a sharp knife, score the round into 8 wedges. Bake in a preheated oven at 220°C (425°F) Gas 7 for about 20–25 minutes until lightly golden and firm to the touch.

Cool on a wire rack. Eat warm, immediately or within 24 hours. The scones are also good split and toasted. When thoroughly cooled, they can be wrapped then frozen for up to 1 month.

1 large cooking apple or 1–2 crisp tart eating apples (about 250 g)

200 g plain flour, plus extra for dusting

80 g wholemeal flour

1 teaspoon bicarbonate of soda

75 g demerara sugar, plus extra for sprinkling

75 g unsalted butter, chilled and diced

about 140 ml buttermilk, plus extra for brushing or milk for brushing

a large baking sheet, greased

Makes 8 scones

treacle bread

350 g wholemeal flour

115 g plain flour

1 teaspoon bicabonate of soda

1 teaspoon sea salt

2 tablespoons sesame seeds

1 teaspoon light muscovado sugar

1 teaspoon ground ginger

25 g unsalted butter, chilled
and diced

1 large egg

300 ml plain yoghurt

1½ tablespoons black treacle

1 tablespoon sesame seeds

a 450 g loaf tin, well greased

Makes 1 medium loaf

Put the flours and bicarbonate of soda in a large bowl, then stir in the salt, sesame seeds, sugar and ginger. Mix well. Rub in the diced butter with your fingertips until the mixture looks like fine crumbs.

Lightly beat the egg with the yoghurt and treacle, then quickly stir into the dry mixture, using a wooden spoon. With floured hands, knead the dough 2–3 times in the bowl so it just comes together. It should be heavy and sticky – quite unlike a scone dough or a yeasted bread dough. If it is too dry or too wet, add extra yoghurt or flour, 1 tablespoon at a time. (The exact amount of liquid needed will depend on the quality of the flour.) Shape the dough into a loaf to fit the tin, then gently roll it in the sesame seeds to cover. Press the dough neatly into the prepared tin.

Bake the loaf in a preheated oven at 200°C (400°F) Gas 6 for 10 minutes, then reduce to 180°C (350°F) Gas 4 and bake for a further 35 minutes. (If it browns too quickly or too much, cover with foil or baking parchment.) The cooked bread should be browned, well risen and should sound hollow when turned out and tapped underneath. If it sounds heavy or the crust is flabby, return the turned-out loaf to the oven for 5 minutes, then test again.

Cool on a wire rack. Although this loaf is good the day it is baked, it tastes even better if wrapped and kept for a day before eating. When thoroughly cooled, the loaf can be wrapped then frozen for up to 1 month.

Cheese is packed with calcium: cottage cheese is the low-fat way to have it – delicious too. Enhance with fresh herbs or dried fruit.

**500 g self-raising flour, plus
extra for dusting**

½ teaspoon sea salt

250 g cottage cheese

1 large egg

about 150 ml milk

extra milk or beaten egg, for glazing

Herb rolls:

3 tablespoons chopped parsley

¼ teaspoon freshly ground black pepper

Fruit rolls:

**2 tablespoons golden caster sugar
or 1 tablespoon honey**

**3 tablespoons dried sour cherries,
cranberries or fresh blueberries**

a large baking sheet, floured

Makes 10 rolls

Put the flour, salt, cottage cheese and egg into a food processor and process until just mixed. With the machine running, add enough milk through the feed tube until the mixture comes together to form a soft but not sticky dough.

Turn out onto a lightly floured surface and knead lightly 2–3 times until smooth. Divide the dough into 10 equal pieces and shape each one into a ball. Arrange, spaced slightly apart, on the floured baking sheet and brush lightly with milk or beaten egg. Bake in a preheated oven at 190°C (375°F) Gas 5 for about 20 minutes until golden brown and firm. Cool on a wire rack. Eat warm, immediately or within 24 hours, or split and toast. When thoroughly cooled, the rolls can be wrapped then frozen for up to 1 month.

Variations:

Herb rolls: Add the parsley and pepper to the food processor with the cottage cheese, then proceed with the recipe.

Fruit rolls: Add the sugar or honey to the processor with the flour. Make the dough, as above. Knead the fruit into it. Proceed as above.

cottage cheese rolls

A variation on the traditional Irish recipe using malted-grains or Granary™ flour. Perfect with smoked salmon and scrambled eggs.

Put the flours, salt and bicarbonate of soda in a large bowl. Rub in the diced butter with your fingertips until the mixture looks like fine crumbs. Make a well in the centre and, using a palette knife or wooden spoon, work in enough buttermilk or yoghurt to form a coarse, stiff dough. Turn out onto a floured surface and knead 2–3 times. Shape into a round loaf about 18 cm across and 3 cm thick. Put on the baking sheet and dust lightly with flour. Cut a fairly deep cross on the surface of the loaf, then bake in a preheated oven at 220°C (425°F) Gas 7 for 25–30 minutes until well risen, with a

malted brown soda bread

350 g malted-grains flour, malted-wheat flour
  or Granary™ flour

100 g plain flour, plus extra for dusting

1 teaspoon sea salt

1 teaspoon bicarbonate of soda

30 g unsalted butter, chilled and diced

300–400 ml buttermilk or plain yoghurt,

a baking sheet, well floured

Makes 1 medium loaf

good, browned crust. The bread should sound hollow when tapped underneath. Cool on a wire rack. Eat within 24 hours, or split and toast. When thoroughly cooled, the soda bread can be wrapped then frozen for up to 1 month.

Variations:

Fruit soda bread: Follow the main recipe, replacing the malted-grains flour with stoneground wholemeal flour. Add 1 tablespoon demerara sugar and 100 g mixed dried fruit to the rubbed-in mixture, then add the buttermilk and proceed with the recipe.

Spotted soda bread: Follow the recipe for fruit soda bread, using 100 g coarsely chopped plain chocolate (choose one with at least 70 per cent or more cocoa solids) instead of the dried fruit.

a large pinch of saffron strands

3–4 tablespoons cold milk

230 g self-raising flour

a pinch of salt

40 g golden caster sugar

40 g unsalted butter, chilled and diced

1 large egg

extra milk or beaten egg, to glaze

a 6-cm plain or fluted biscuit cutter

a baking sheet, lightly greased

Makes 8 scones

For the lightest, fluffiest scones, make them in a food processor and handle the mixture as little as possible. Eat with butter and honey.

Put the saffron in a heatproof ramekin dish and toast in a preheated oven at 180°C (350°F) Gas 4 for about 10–15 minutes until slightly darkened but not scorched. Cool for 1 minute, then crumble the strands back into the dish, add 2 tablespoons of the milk, cover and let soak overnight or at least 4 hours.

Mix the flour, salt and sugar in a food processor. Add the butter and process until the mixture looks like fine crumbs. Beat the egg with the saffron milk, then with the machine running, slowly pour the liquid through the feed tube to bring the mixture together to make a soft but not sticky dough. If the dough seems dry and won't come together, add 1–2 tablespoons milk. Turn out onto a lightly floured surface, then pat or roll out to about 2 cm thick. Dip the biscuit cutter in flour and stamp out as many rounds as possible. Gather the trimmings into a ball, pat out again and cut out more rounds. Repeat until all the dough has been used.

Put the scones well apart on the baking sheet. They can be left plain, dusted lightly with flour or glazed with a little milk or beaten egg. Bake in a preheated oven at 220°C (425°F) Gas 7 for about 12 minutes until well risen, golden and just firm. Cool on a wire rack. Eat warm, on the day of baking, or split and toast. When thoroughly cooled, the scones can be wrapped then frozen for up to 1 month.

Variation:
Blue Cheese Scones: Omit the sugar. Knead 60 g crumbled Stilton or Shropshire Blue cheese (avoid Danish Blue as it is too salty) into the dough with 40 g walnut pieces, then continue as above.

saffron scones

french toast

4 slices thick-cut white bread, challah or brioche

2 large eggs, beaten

2 tablespoons single cream or top of the milk

$\frac{1}{2}$ teaspoon pure vanilla essence

$3\frac{1}{2}$ tablespoons golden caster sugar

about 50 g butter, for frying

$\frac{1}{2}$ teaspoon ground cinnamon

maple syrup, to serve (optional)

Serves 4

Trim the crusts from the bread, then cut the slices in half. Put the eggs, cream, vanilla essence and 1 teaspoon of the sugar in a shallow dish and mix with a fork.

Heat half the butter in a large, heavy, cast-iron or non-stick frying pan. When the butter is foaming, briefly dip a piece of bread in the egg mixture until thoroughly coated, drain off the excess and put it in the hot butter. Add 3 more pieces of coated bread to the pan in the same way, then cook over a medium heat for 3–4 minutes until the underside is golden brown. Turn the bread over and cook the other side. Meanwhile, mix the remaining sugar and cinnamon in a small sugar shaker or bowl. Put the cooked bread on a warm serving plate and sprinkle with some of the cinnamon sugar.

Wipe out the frying pan and reheat. Add the rest of the butter and cook the other pieces of bread as before. Serve hot as soon as possible, sprinkled with more cinnamon sugar and maple syrup, if using.

cinnamon toast

The quickest, simplest breakfast treat ever invented, but it does demand top-quality ingredients – good white bread, unsalted butter and the best ground cinnamon. Heat the grill, toast thick slices of bread on both sides, then butter thoroughly. Mix the cinnamon sugar, as in the previous recipe, and sprinkle generously to cover. Put the toast back under the grill until the sugar starts to melt and bubble. Remove carefully and eat when the toast has cooled enough not to burn your lips (the top will look like a brandy snap – lacy and crisp).

american pancakes

Sift the flour, salt and sugar into a bowl, then make a well in the centre. Add the egg yolks, butter and milk and beat with a whisk until mixed. Gradually work in the flour to make a very thick but lump-free batter. In another bowl, whisk the egg whites until stiff, then fold them into the batter with a large metal spoon. Heat a heavy-based frying pan until medium hot, then grease it lightly with butter.

Fry the mixture in batches of 3, using a heaped tablespoon of batter for each pancake. Cook for about 1 minute until golden underneath, then turn over with a spatula and cook for another minute. Serve hot with maple syrup.

120 g plain flour

a good pinch of salt

1 tablespoon golden caster sugar

2 large eggs, separated

20 g unsalted butter, melted, plus extra for frying

200 ml full-fat milk

maple syrup, to serve

Makes 12 pancakes

Serves 4

waffles

Make the batter as for the pancakes, but use just 1 egg and add $1\frac{1}{2}$ teaspoons baking powder with the flour and $\frac{1}{2}$ teaspoon of pure vanilla essence with the milk.

Crisp waffles or fluffy, thick pancakes drizzled with maple syrup make a good breakfast.

Using a non-plastic pastry brush, thoroughly grease a waffle iron or electric waffle maker with a little corn oil or melted butter, then heat (according to the maker's instructions). Pour in enough batter to fill, then close and cook over medium heat for 30 seconds. Turn the waffle iron over and cook the other side for 30 seconds. For an electric waffle maker, follow the manufacturer's guidelines for cooking. Dust the hot waffles with icing sugar and eat immediately, drizzled with maple syrup, or omit the icing sugar and serve with eggs and crispy bacon.

Serves 4

A coffee cake in name only – meant to be enjoyed with a cup of coffee.

115 g unsalted butter, at room temperature

170 g light muscovado sugar

250 g plain flour

2 teaspoons bicarbonate of soda

2 large eggs

250 ml sour cream

Filling and topping:

3 tablespoons dark muscovado sugar

1 tablespoon ground cinnamon

90 g walnut pieces

a 1 kg loaf tin, greased and base-lined

Makes 1 large loaf cake

Using an electric mixer or wooden spoon, beat the butter until light and creamy. Add the sugar – sift it first if it appears lumpy – and beat again until light and fluffy. Sift the flour and bicarbonate of soda onto the creamed butter mixture. Stir once or twice, then quickly beat the eggs with the sour cream and add to the bowl. Using a rubber spatula or wooden spoon, stir all the ingredients together to make a soft, smooth batter.

Mix the filling and topping ingredients. Spoon half the cake batter into the prepared loaf tin, then sprinkle over half the filling and topping mixture. Spoon the rest of the cake batter on top and smooth the surface. Sprinkle over the rest of the filling and topping mixture, then press lightly onto the surface of the loaf.

Bake in a preheated oven at 180°C (350°F) Gas 4 for about 45 minutes to 1 hour until lightly browned and firm and a skewer inserted into the centre comes out clean. Let cool in the tin for 5 minutes, then carefully turn out onto a wire rack. Serve warm. The cake is best eaten within 3 days. When thoroughly cooled, it can be wrapped then frozen for up to 1 month.

sour cream coffee cake

loaf cakes

Light and crumbly in texture, crammed with delicious fruit and nuts – irresistible. Use very ripe bananas for maximum flavour.

banana pecan loaf

Using an electric mixer or wooden spoon, beat the butter with the sugar until light and creamy. Gradually beat in the eggs and vanilla essence to make a fluffy mixture. Mash the bananas with a fork – they should be fairly coarse rather than a purée. Carefully fold in the mashed bananas, pecans and flour. Transfer the mixture to the prepared loaf tin and smooth the surface with a palette knife. Bake in a preheated oven at 180°C (350°F) Gas 4 for about 1 hour until golden and firm to the touch and a skewer inserted into the centre comes out clean.

Let cool in the tin for 5 minutes, then turn out onto a wire rack to cool completely. Serve warm or at room temperature, thickly sliced and spread with butter. The cake is best eaten within 3 days. When thoroughly cooled, it can be wrapped then frozen for up to 1 month.

125 g unsalted butter,
   at room temperature

170 g golden caster sugar

2 large eggs, beaten

½ teaspoon pure vanilla essence

400 g very ripe bananas

100 g pecans, coarsely sliced

250 g self-raising flour, sifted

a 1 kg loaf tin, greased and
   base-lined

Makes 1 large loaf cake

dorset apple cake

I adore the simple, fresh taste of this easy loaf cake – perfect when you need an energy boost and crave something uncomplicated.

Using an electric mixer or wooden spoon, beat the butter until creamy, then add the sugar and beat until light and fluffy. Gradually beat in the eggs, then the vanilla essence. Using a large metal spoon, fold in the flour and enough milk to make a soft mixture that just drops from the spoon. Transfer the mixture to the prepared loaf tin and smooth the surface with a palette knife. Arrange an even layer of apple slices over the top.

To make the topping, put all the ingredients into a mixing bowl and rub together with your fingertips until the mixture looks like coarse crumbs. (The ingredients can also be mixed in a food processor.) Sprinkle the topping evenly over the apples, then press down gently to firm. Bake in a preheated oven at 180°C (350°F) Gas 4 for about 1 hour until golden and a skewer inserted into the centre comes out clean.

Let cool in the tin until lukewarm, then serve warm from the tin or cool completely on a wire rack. Eat within 3 days. When thoroughly cooled, the loaf cake can be wrapped then frozen for up to 1 month.

100 g unsalted butter, at room temperature
100 g golden caster sugar
2 large eggs, beaten
½ teaspoon pure vanilla essence
150 g self-raising flour, sifted
2–3 tablespoons milk
2 medium Bramleys or 3 tart eating apples (about 380 g), peeled, cored and thickly sliced

Topping:
75 g demerara sugar
75 g unsalted butter, chilled and diced
150 g plain flour, sifted

a 450 g loaf tin, greased and base-lined

Makes 1 medium loaf cake

1 firm, slightly underripe pear

230 g self-raising flour

1 teaspoon bicarbonate of soda

1 tablespoon ground ginger

1 teaspoon ground cinnamon

1 teaspoon ground mixed spice

1/8 teaspoon ground black pepper

115 g unsalted butter, chilled and diced

115 g black treacle

115 g golden syrup

115 g dark muscovado sugar

280 ml milk

1 large egg, beaten

a 1 kg loaf tin, greased and base-lined

Makes 1 large loaf cake

Peel, core and dice the pear into 1 cm pieces. Set aside. Sift the flour, bicarbonate of soda and spices into a large bowl. Rub in the diced butter with your fingertips until the mixture looks like fine crumbs. Alternatively, you can use a food processor.

Put the treacle and syrup in a small saucepan, melt over low heat, then cool until lukewarm. Dissolve the sugar in the milk over low heat, stirring frequently, then let cool until lukewarm.

Whisk the milk into the flour mixture, quickly followed by the treacle mixture and the egg. When the mixture is smooth and lump-free, pour it into the prepared tin. Top with the diced pear – the pieces will slowly sink as they cook.

Bake the gingerbread in a preheated oven at 180°C (350°F) Gas 4 for 45 minutes to 1 hour until well risen and firm to the touch and a skewer inserted into the centre comes out clean. Let cool completely in the tin, then turn out. Serve warm or at room temperature, thickly sliced. The gingerbread is best eaten within 2 days and is not suitable for freezing.

pear gingerbread

Pears and ginger go hand-in-hand in this deliciously rich cake.

For a full tea-flavour, use a strong variety such as a breakfast or Irish blend, or a rich malty Assam. Eat the loaf cake thickly sliced, warm or even toasted, with or without butter and jam.

breakfast tea loaf

100 g shredded bran cereal

120 g dark muscovado sugar

130 g mixed dried fruit

175 ml strong tea, warm

30 g walnut pieces

100 g plain flour, sifted

1½ teaspoons baking powder

1½ teaspoons ground mixed spice

a 450 g loaf tin, greased and base-lined

Makes 1 medium loaf cake

Put the cereal, sugar and dried fruit into a large bowl, add the warm tea, stir well, then cover and let soak for 30 minutes.

Add the remaining ingredients, and stir with a wooden spoon until thoroughly mixed. (The cereal will disappear into the mixture.)

Spoon the mixture into the prepared loaf tin and smooth the surface with a palette knife. Bake in a preheated oven at 180°C (350°F) Gas 4 for about 45 minutes until firm and well risen and a skewer inserted into the centre comes out clean.

Let cool in the tin until lukewarm, then turn out and eat while still warm. Alternatively, turn out onto a wire rack to cool completely.

The loaf cake is best if wrapped and kept for a day before cutting. Eat within 4 days, or wrap then freeze for up to 1 month.

carrot and almond loaf cake

Everyone loves a carrot cake – this one is moist and packed with creamy, crunchy almonds. Delicious anytime of the morning.

Put the flour, all the almonds, lemon rind and carrots in a large bowl and mix well with a wooden spoon.

Whisk the egg yolks with half the sugar until very thick and fluffy. In another, spotlessly clean, grease-free bowl, whisk the egg whites until stiff peaks form, then gradually whisk in the sugar to form a meringue. Using a large metal spoon, gently fold the carrot mixture into the whisked yolk mixture, followed by the meringue. (There should be no trace of meringue visible in the mixture.)

Spoon the mixture into the prepared loaf tin and smooth the surface. Bake in a preheated oven at 180°C (350°F) Gas 4 for about 1 hour until golden and firm to the touch and a skewer inserted into the centre comes out clean. Let cool in the tin until lukewarm, then turn out onto a wire rack to cool completely. The loaf cake is best eaten within 2 days and is not suitable for freezing.

100 g self-raising flour, sifted

300 g ground almonds

50 g whole blanched almonds, very coarsely ground, or flaked almonds

grated rind of 1 small unwaxed lemon

200 g grated carrots (about 250 g before peeling and trimming)

6 large eggs, separated

200 g light muscovado sugar

a 1 kg loaf tin, greased and base-lined

Makes 1 large loaf cake

les petits pains au lait

Gently heat the butter, honey and milk in a small saucepan until the butter melts. Let cool until lukewarm – blood heat or cooler – then crumble in the yeast and whisk until smooth. Mix the flour and salt in a large bowl, then make a well in the centre. Pour in the yeast liquid and the eggs, then work in the flour to make a soft but not sticky dough. If it is too dry or too sticky, add extra water or flour, 1 tablespoon at a time. Turn out onto a lightly floured surface and knead thoroughly for 10 minutes (or 6 minutes at medium speed in a mixer fitted with a dough hook). Return the dough to the bowl and cover with a damp tea towel or put the bowl in an oiled plastic bag. Let rise at normal room temperature until doubled in size – about 2 hours.

Knock down the risen dough with your knuckles, turn out and knead lightly. Cut into 16 even-sized pieces and shape into ovals, 10 x 6 x 1 cm. Set well apart on the baking sheets, cover and let rise as before until doubled in size – about 1 hour. Brush with beaten egg or milk to glaze and sprinkle with the sugar. Using a sharp knife, make a long shallow slit down the length of each roll. Bake in a preheated oven at 220°C (425°F) Gas 7 for 12–15 minutes until the rolls are browned and sound hollow when tapped underneath. Cool on a wire rack. Eat warm, within 24 hours, or split and toast. When thoroughly cooled, the rolls can be wrapped then frozen for up to 1 month.

To use easy-blend dried yeast, mix one 7 g sachet with the flour and salt. Make a well in the centre, add the butter, milk and honey mixture and eggs, then proceed with the recipe.

70 g unsalted butter

1½ tablespoons honey

350 ml milk

15 g fresh yeast*

750 g strong white bread flour, sifted

2 teaspoons sea salt

3 large eggs, beaten

extra beaten egg or milk, for brushing

demerara sugar, for sprinkling

2 large baking sheets, greased

Makes 16 rolls

yeasted breads

Great for a fast, simple breakfast – on its own or toasted and buttered. Cinnamon, raisins and nuts are a classic combination.

650 g strong white bread flour

1½ tablespoons ground cinnamon

1 teaspoon sea salt

1 teaspoon light muscovado sugar

100 g unsalted butter, chilled and diced

15 g fresh yeast*

425 ml milk, at room temperature

100 g raisins

75 g walnut pieces, lightly toasted

a large baking sheet, greased

Makes 1 large loaf

cinnamon raisin nut bread

Sift the flour, cinnamon, salt and sugar into a large bowl. Rub in the butter with your fingertips until the mixture looks like fine crumbs, then make a well in the centre. Crumble the yeast into a jug and whisk in the milk. Pour into the well and mix in enough flour to make a thick batter. Cover the bowl and leave until thick and foamy – about 20 minutes.

Work in the rest of the flour to make a soft but not sticky dough. If it is too dry or too sticky, add extra water or flour, 1 tablespoon at a time. Turn out onto a floured surface and knead thoroughly for 10 minutes (or 6 minutes at medium speed in a mixer fitted with a dough hook) until smooth and elastic. Return to the bowl, cover with a damp tea towel and let rise at normal room temperature until doubled in size – about 1½ hours.

Knock down the risen dough with your knuckles, then work in the fruit and nuts, kneading until thoroughly mixed. Shape the dough into an oval loaf about 25 x 15 cm. Put on the prepared baking sheet, cover and let rise as before until doubled in size – about 45 minutes.

Bake in a preheated oven at 220°C (425°F) Gas 7 for about 35 minutes until the bread is nicely browned and sounds hollow when tapped underneath. Cool on a wire rack. Eat within 4 days, or slice and toast. The cooled loaf can be wrapped then frozen for up to 1 month.

*To use easy-blend dried yeast, mix one 7 g sachet with 100 g of the sifted flour mixture. Mix to a thick batter with the milk, cover and leave until thick and foamy. Rub the butter into the remaining flour, add the frothy yeast mixture and proceed with the recipe.

sticky buns

Mix the flour, salt and sugar in a large bowl and make a well in the centre. Crumble the fresh yeast into another bowl, add the lukewarm milk and stir until blended. Pour the yeast liquid into the well, then work in enough of the flour to make a thick batter. Cover the bowl with a damp tea towel and leave until foamy, thick and full of air bubbles – about 15 minutes.

Add the butter and egg to the yeast mixture and work in the rest of the flour to make a soft but not sticky dough. If it is too dry or too sticky, add extra water or flour, 1 tablespoon at a time. Turn out onto a lightly floured surface and knead thoroughly for 10 minutes (or 6 minutes at medium speed in a mixer fitted with a dough hook). Return the dough to the bowl and cover with a damp tea towel or put the bowl in an oiled plastic bag. Let rise at normal room temperature until doubled in size – about 1½ hours.

Knock down the risen dough with your knuckles, then turn out and roll into a rectangle, about 40 x 25 cm.

To make the filling, beat the butter until creamy, then beat in the cinnamon and sugar. Spread the mixture over the dough leaving a 5-mm border around the edges. Scatter the nuts over, then roll into a 40-cm-long roll. Cut into 12 equal pieces and space slightly apart in the tin, in 4 rows of 3. Cover and let rise as before until doubled in size – about 30 minutes (or chill overnight).

Put the topping ingredients in a small saucepan, bring to the boil, reduce the heat and simmer for 1 minute. Pour the hot mixture over the buns. Bake in a preheated oven at 200°C (400°F) Gas 6 for 25–30 minutes until golden and firm. Let cool in the tin for 10 minutes, then turn out carefully – the caramel will be hot. Cool on a wire rack. Eat warm or at room temperature, within 24 hours. The buns are not suitable for freezing.

To use easy-blend dried yeast mix one 7 g sachet with 100 g of the flour. Mix with the warm milk, cover and leave until thick and foamy. Mix the remaining flour with the sugar and salt, add the frothy yeast mixture, egg and butter, then proceed with the recipe.

An all-time family favourite – who can resist these gooey, sticky caramel buns filled with cinnamon and nuts?

500 g strong white bread flour, sifted

1 teaspoon sea salt

40 g golden caster sugar

15 g fresh yeast*

about 200 ml milk, lukewarm

50 g unsalted butter, melted

1 large egg, beaten

Nut caramel filling:

60 g unsalted butter, very soft

2 teaspoons ground cinnamon

50 g light muscovado sugar

100 g pecans or walnut halves
   or pieces

Sticky topping:

90 g light muscovado sugar

4 tablespoons double cream

a 22 x 28 x 4 cm baking or
   roasting tin, well greased

Makes 12 buns

sour cherry brioche

500 g strong white bread flour, sifted

1½ teaspoons sea salt

15 g fresh yeast*

75 ml milk, lukewarm

6 large eggs, beaten

200 g unsalted butter, very soft

3 tablespoons golden caster sugar

75 g dried sour cherries

extra beaten egg or milk, to glaze

a 23-cm springform tin, well greased

Makes 1 large loaf

Mix the flour and salt in an electric mixer or large bowl. Make a well in the centre. Crumble the yeast into a large measuring jug, whisk in the lukewarm milk until smooth, then whisk in the eggs. Pour into the well and mix with a dough hook or by hand to make a smooth, soft and sticky dough. Knead until firm, silky and elastic – about 6–7 minutes with a dough hook on medium-low speed, or 10 minutes by hand. Cover with a damp tea towel, or upside-down bowl and let rest for 10 minutes.

Meanwhile, beat the butter with the sugar until creamy, then work in the dried cherries. Gradually work the butter mixture into the dough, a little at a time, beating at low speed with the dough hook or squeezing the butter and dough together with your hands. Work the dough for 2 minutes until smooth and glossy. Cover the bowl with a damp tea towel or put it in an oiled plastic bag. Let rise at normal room temperature until doubled in size – about 2 hours.

Knock down the risen dough with your knuckles to flatten, cover and chill for at least 12 hours or overnight. The dough must be thoroughly chilled or it will be difficult to handle and shape.

Turn out the dough onto a lightly floured surface and divide into 18 equal pieces. Shape into neat balls and arrange in the prepared tin to resemble a crown. Cover and let rise as before until doubled in size – about 45 minutes to 1 hour.

To glaze the brioche, brush it with beaten egg or milk. Bake in a preheated oven at 220°C (425°F) Gas 7 for about 35 minutes until well risen, golden brown and firm. It should sound hollow when turned out and tapped underneath. (If it browns too quickly or too much, cover with foil or baking parchment.) Cool on a wire rack. Serve warm, within 2 days, or slice and toast. When thoroughly cooled, the brioche can be wrapped then frozen for up to 1 month.

To use easy-blend dried yeast, mix one 7 g sachet with the flour and salt. Whisk the eggs and milk together, then proceed with the recipe.

Halve the apricots, then put them in a heatproof bowl with the honey and pour over 140 ml very hot water. Stir well, then set aside and leave, uncovered, until the water is tepid and the honey has dissolved.

Mix the flours in a large bowl and add the salt. Make a well in the centre. Crumble the yeast into a small jug and whisk in the milk until blended. Pour into the well with the melted butter or oil, then add the apricots and their soaking liquid. Mix in the flour to make a soft but not sticky dough. If the dough is too dry or too sticky, add extra water or flour, 1 tablespoon at a time.

Work in the nuts, then turn out the dough onto a lightly floured surface and knead thoroughly for 10 minutes. Return to the bowl and cover with a damp tea towel or put the bowl in an oiled plastic bag. Let rise at normal room temperature until doubled in size – about 1½ hours. Knock down the risen dough with your knuckles, then turn out onto a surface dusted with rye flour. Shape into a loaf and press gently into the tin. Cover and let rise as before at normal room temperature until doubled in size – about 1 hour.

Bake in a preheated oven at 220°C (425°F) Gas 7 for 35–40 minutes until the loaf is golden brown and sounds hollow when turned out and tapped underneath. Cool on a wire rack. It is best eaten within 4 days, or sliced and toasted. Serve with butter, preserves, honey or cheese. When thoroughly cooled, the loaf can be wrapped then frozen for up to 1 month.

100 g no-need-to-soak dried apricots

2 tablespoons well-flavoured honey

400 g strong white bread flour, sifted

100 g rye flour, plus extra for dusting

2 teaspoons sea salt

15 g fresh yeast*

140 g milk, at room temperature

2 tablespoons melted butter or olive oil

100 g hazelnuts, toasted and halved

a 1 kg loaf tin, greased

Makes 1 large loaf

*To use easy-blend dried yeast, mix one 7 g sachet with the flours and salt. Add the milk, butter and apricot mixture, then proceed with the recipe.

apricot and honey rye bread

Delicious lightly buttered and topped with honey, preserves or cheese.

double chocolate kugelhopf

A pretty, very rich yeast cake from Austria, Germany and Alsace – a luxurious breakfast or mid-morning treat.

To make the nut coating, thickly butter the inside of the mould (glazed earthenware, non-stick, heatproof glass, or metal), then press the almonds all around. Chill while you prepare the cake dough.

To make the dough, sift the flour, cocoa, salt and sugar into a large bowl and make a well in the centre. Crumble the yeast into a small bowl and add the lukewarm milk. Whisk to make a smooth liquid. Pour into the well, then work in enough of the flour to make a thick batter. Cover with a damp tea towel and leave at normal room temperature for 30 minutes. The batter should look thick and bubbly.

Add the eggs to the batter, mix well, then gradually beat in the flour to make a soft, very sticky dough. Beat the

Nut coating:

25 g unsalted butter, very soft

50 g flaked almonds

350 g strong white bread flour

50 g unsweetened cocoa powder

½ teaspoon sea salt

100 g caster sugar

15 g fresh yeast*

200 ml milk, lukewarm

3 large eggs, at room
    temperature, beaten

100 g unsalted butter,
    very soft

50 g slivered or
    flaked almonds

60 g white chocolate,
    coarsely chopped

icing sugar, for dusting

a 23-cm kugelhopf mould

Makes 1 large cake

dough in the bowl using your hand or with the dough hook in an electric mixer for about 5 minutes or until firm, smooth, very elastic and shiny. Work in the butter, a little at a time, until thoroughly incorporated, then work in the almonds and white chocolate. When evenly mixed, carefully spoon the soft dough into the prepared kugelhopf mould. It should be half-full.

Cover the mould with a damp tea towel and let rise at normal room temperature until the dough has risen to about 2.5 cm below the rim – about 1 hour.

Bake the kugelhopf in a preheated oven at 200°C (400°F) Gas 6 for about 45 minutes or until a skewer inserted into the cake, midway between the outer edge and inner tube, comes out clean. Cool for 2 minutes, then carefully turn out onto a wire rack and let cool completely. Serve dusted with icing sugar. It is best eaten within 3 days, or sliced and lightly toasted. When thoroughly cooled, the kugelhopf can be wrapped then frozen for up to 1 month.

To use easy-blend dried yeast, mix one 7 g sachet with about 140 g of the flour mixture. Mix in the milk to make a smooth batter, cover and leave for about 30 minutes until thick and foamy. Make a well in the remaining flour mixture, add the frothy yeast mixture and eggs, and proceed with the recipe.

1 teaspoon saffron strands

500 g strong white bread flour, sifted

1 teaspoon sea salt

180 g unsalted butter,
   chilled and diced

15 g fresh yeast*

180 ml milk, lukewarm, plus
   extra, for brushing

2 tablespoons honey

a 1 kg loaf tin, greased

Makes 1 large loaf

saffron and honey bread

Well-flavoured but not over-sweet – wonderful spread with butter and fruit preserves, or toasted and served with ham and eggs.

Put the saffron in a heatproof ramekin dish and toast in a preheated oven at 180°C (350°F) Gas 4 for about 10–15 minutes until dark but not scorched. Cool, then add 3 tablespoons water, cover and let soak overnight.

The next day, mix the flour and salt in a large bowl. Rub in the diced butter with your fingertips until the mixture looks like fine crumbs. Make a well in the centre. Crumble the yeast into a small jug, then whisk in the milk and honey to make a smooth liquid. Pour into the well, followed by the saffron liquid. Mix with your hand to make a soft but not sticky dough.

Turn out onto a floured surface and knead thoroughly for 10 minutes (or 6 minutes at medium speed in a mixer fitted with a dough hook) until smooth, silky and elastic. Return to the bowl, cover with a damp tea towel or put it in an oiled plastic bag and let rise at normal room temperature until doubled in size – about 1½ hours.

Knock down the risen dough with your knuckles, turn out onto a lightly floured surface and shape into a loaf to fit the tin. Press the dough neatly into the prepared tin. Cover and let rise as before until doubled in size – about 1 hour.

Brush the risen loaf with milk, then bake in a preheated oven at 190°C (375°F) Gas 5 for 30 minutes until lightly browned. Reduce the temperature to 180°C (350°F) Gas 4 and bake for a further 15–20 minutes until the turned-out loaf sounds hollow when tapped underneath. (If it browns too quickly or too much, cover with foil.) Cool on a wire rack. It is best eaten within 4 days, or sliced and toasted. When thoroughly cooled, the loaf can be wrapped then frozen for up to 1 month.

*To use easy-blend dried yeast, mix one 7 g sachet with the flour and salt, rub in the butter to look like fine crumbs, add the milk and honey, then proceed with the recipe.

750 g strong white bread flour, sifted, plus extra,
   for dusting
3 teaspoons sea salt
15 g fresh yeast*
about 450 ml buttermilk, at room temperature

a large baking sheet, greased

Makes 1 large loaf

Cultured buttermilk gives white flour a distinctive tang. This loaf has rustic, country appeal.

Put the flour and salt in a large bowl and make a well in the centre. Crumble the fresh yeast into a small bowl, mix to a smooth paste with 1 tablespoon lukewarm water, then stir in the buttermilk. Pour the yeast liquid into the well and gradually work in the flour to make a soft dough. If the dough is too sticky or too dry, add more flour or lukewarm water, 1 tablespoon at a time.

Turn out the dough onto a floured work surface and knead thoroughly for 10 minutes (or 6 minutes at medium speed in a mixer fitted with a dough hook). Return to the bowl and cover with a damp tea towel or put it in an oiled plastic bag and let rise at normal room temperature until doubled in size – about 1½ hours.

Knock down the risen dough with your knuckles. Turn out onto a lighly floured surface, knead briefly and shape into a ball. Lightly dust with flour. Put on the prepared baking sheet, cover and let rise as before until doubled in size – 45 minutes to 1 hour. Using a very sharp knife, score the top in a criss-cross pattern, as pictured. Bake in a preheated oven at 220°C (425°F) Gas 7 for 40 minutes until the loaf is golden and sounds hollow when tapped underneath. Cool on a wire rack. It is best eaten within 3 days, or sliced and toasted. When thoroughly cooled, the loaf can be wrapped then frozen for up to 1 month.

*To use easy-blend dried yeast, mix one 7 g sachet with the flour and salt, then proceed with the recipe.

buttermilk hedgehog loaf

Almond:
  carrot and, loaf cake 46
  lemon, and blueberry muffins 12
American pancakes 34
apple:
  buttermilk scone round 22
  Dorset, cake 40
apricot and honey rye bread 56

Bacon muffins, cornmeal and 18
banana pecan loaf 38
baps, oat 20
blue cheese scones 30
blueberry muffins, lemon, almond
    and 12
bran:
  breakfast tea loaf 44
  cardamom, carrot and, muffins 8
breakfast tea loaf 44
brioche, sour cherry 54
buns, sticky 52
buttermilk
  apple, scone round 22
  fresh peach and oat muffins 16
  fruit soda bread 28
  hedgehog loaf 62
  malted brown soda bread 28
  spotted soda bread 28

Cardamom, carrot and bran
    muffins 8
carrot
  and almond loaf cake 46
  cardamom, and bran muffins 8
cinnamon:
  raisin nut bread 50
  sticky buns 52
  toast 32
cheese:
  cottage, rolls 26
  blue, scones 30
chocolate:
  double, kugelhopf 58
  spotted soda bread 28
coffee cake, sour cream 36
cornmeal and bacon muffins 18
cottage cheese rolls 26
cranberry muffins, pecan, orange
    and 14

Dorset apple cake 40
double chocolate kugelhopf 58

French toast 32
fresh peach and oat muffins 16
fruit:
  apple buttermilk scone round
    22
  apricot and honey rye bread 56
  banana pecan loaf 38
  breakfast tea loaf 44
  cinnamon raisin nut bread 50
  Dorset apple cake 40
  fresh peach and oat muffins 16
  lemon, almond and blueberry
    muffins 12
  pear gingerbread 42
  pecan, orange and cranberry
    muffins 14
  rolls 26
  soda bread 28
  sour cherry brioche 54

Gingerbread, pear 42

Hedgehog loaf, buttermilk 62
herb rolls 26
honey:
  apricot and, rye bread 56
  saffron and, bread 60

Kugelhopf, double chocolate 58

Lemon, almond and blueberry
    muffins 12
les petits pains au lait 48
loaf cakes:
  banana pecan 38
  breakfast tea 44
  carrot and almond 46
  Dorset apple cake 40
  pear gingerbread 42

Malted brown soda bread 28
marmalade muffins 10
muffins:
  cardamom, carrot and bran 8
  cornmeal and bacon 18
  fresh peach and oat 16

lemon, almond and blueberry 12
marmalade 10

Nuts:
  banana pecan loaf 38
  breakfast tea loaf 44
  carrot and almond loaf cake 46
  cinnamon raisin nut bread 50
  double chocolate kugelhopf 58
  lemon, almond and blueberry
    muffins 12
  pecan, orange and cranberry
    muffins 14
  sticky buns 52

Oats:
  baps 20
  fresh peach and, muffins 16
orange, pecan and cranberry muffins
    14

Pancakes, American 34
pains au lait 48
pecan:
  banana, loaf 38
  orange and cranberry muffins 14
  sticky buns 52
peach, fresh, and oat muffins 16
pear gingerbread 42
pecan, orange and cranberry
    muffins 14

Quick breads:
  American pancakes 34
  apple buttermilk scone round 22
  cinnamon toast 32
  cottage cheese rolls 26
  French toast 32
  malted brown soda bread 28
  oat baps 20
  saffron scones 30
  treacle bread 24
  waffles 35

Raisin nut bread, cinnamon 50
rolls:
  cottage cheese 26
  fruit 26
  herb 26

les petits pains au lait 48
oat baps 20
rye bread, apricot and honey 56

Scones:
  apple buttermilk scone round 22
  blue cheese 30
  saffron 30
saffron:
  and honey bread 60
  scones 30
soda bread:
  fruit 28
  malted brown 28
  spotted 28
sour cherry brioche 54
sour cream coffee cake 36
spotted soda bread 28
sticky buns 52

Tea loaf, breakfast 44
toast:
  cinnamon 32
  French 32
treacle bread 24

Waffles 35

Yeasted breads:
  apricot and honey rye bread 56
  buttermilk hedgehog loaf 62
  cinnamon raisin nut bread 50
  les petits pains au lait 48
  double chocolate kugelhopf 58
  saffron and honey bread 60
  sour cherry brioche 54
  sticky buns 52